# Nature/Nurture

## Alexandra Olmedo

Nature/Nurture © 2024 Alexandra Olmedo

All rights reserved.

No part of this publication may be reproduced, stored in a retrieval system, or transmitted, in any form or by any means, electronic, mechanical, photocopying, recording or otherwise, without the prior written permission of the presenters.

Alexandra Olmedo asserts the moral right to be identified as author of this work.

Presentation by *BookLeaf Publishing*

Web: www.bookleafpub.com

E-mail: info@bookleafpub.com

ISBN: 9789360941376

First edition 2024

*To all of you who create the perfect environment for me to germinate.*

# ACKNOWLEDGEMENT

I'd like to thank Ralph, my neighbor for inspiring me every Sunday from his garden.
And of course, to those of you who dig holes, plant me, cover me with mulch, and water me until I dare to grow.
And to you, dear Solnuschka, my sunshine.

# PREFACE

One day sitting alone at the window facing my garden, I saw my neighbor of 85 years old working in his lawn; cutting the grass so short that the dry southern California dirt shone through. Then he brought out a sprinkler and began to water the garden, trimmed the orange trees and blew all the leaves from the long concrete driveway into a big trash bag to be collected the following day. As I watched him labor over all these tasks it was like the earth broke through my psyche and started laughing, jesting with gritted teeth, "Why do bother with such menial tasks, when nature does all this so effortlessly without your help?"
This revelation led me down a mental journey of examining the ways in which humans meddle, for lack of better phrase, with nature and the environment around us. Why do we put so much effort into manicuring our properties with such extreme detail without ever truly paying attention to what the land itself may truly need?
Nature/Nurture was the result of this examination in my mind; a dialogue between a personified Humanity and Nature, and how they reconcile their coexistence.

I hope you enjoy reading as much as I enjoyed writing this collection; and may you always be humbled in the presence of Nature and her disposition.

# Intellect

Intellect, but as dandelion seeds floating
aimlessly through the chain-link fence
Down into the over manicured yards and pristine
brick pathways up to red cottage doors and
welcome mats
Intellect, but as waves rolling and crashing,
disturbing the buoys that block the ships from
getting too close to shore
Intellect, but as the moon rising and the stars
shining through the darkened window
brightening the path to your closed bedroom
door
Intellect, but as an apology,
A eulogy,
A proposal or a sign from God
Intellect, but as a distilled experience
and not a yardstick for human progression

# The Gardener

The stems emerge from the gruesome untilled
ground and she nods to the gardener
Making a living tending to something most
cyclical,
Natural,
Hands meddling with the soil adding scraps of
death and other discarded things to create a lush
season for us humans to enjoy
But I've seen the dandelions in the cracks and
the sunflowers in the abandoned parking lots and
the unabashed service they provide,
transforming the liminal into a nourishing
sanctuary with the least effort at all,
And I wonder if the gardener prides himself as
such, as he measures the depth of the holes for
the bulbs and the precise rows for the carrots,
Or if the flowers laugh at him like a knowing
mother watching her child pick up a spoon for
the first time instead of using his hands to eat

# An Land Long Past

The wood creaks and the teeth gnaw at the
fragile posts beneath my bed
The lifeless trees and I sit and listen
My mind leaves me again,
Out the window into the moonlight, floating
through the clouds and into insanity while others
sleep soundly under their in-tact roofs that they
no doubt pay for
Me? I quite enjoy listening to the secrets the
jasmine bushes tell to the coyotes,
And somehow a deep earthly growl resonates
from a land long past
And under millions of miles of rubble is a
collection of all the dead thoughts I once had.
The squirrels and mice like to collect them all
and adorn their hearths with them like wreaths
celebrating some silly rite of passage,
cobble them into their own personal Pompeii fit
with hopes and dreams and civility
While I sit in silence under the ash and weep

# Presenting Like Gasoline

Suddenly the once crystal clear photographs
accumulate the grain of the 90's
The photos of acquaintances and lovers and
fascinating in-betweeners a relic of the
foreverness that was promised to me in my 20's
suddenly displaying the greenish bile-colored
tarnish of disappointment again and again,
Aging naturally like wine but presenting like
gasoline
(at what point does time create a delicacy vs a
poison?)
I remember your freckles then, and bright green
eyes that promised a life with a home and kids
and shiny new things that one could only
promise with a family surname of Audacity
But at night in secret, my dreams developed in
the darkroom of hidden suburban adolescence
and just enough shelter to house the four
horsemen of the apocalypse
The light would shine through though, and the
beams created small burns in crescent moon
shapes and small maps across my back that I
followed aimlessly instead of doing my
homework

# Painting

As you mixed the black and white paints
together on the cold white canvas, did you also
imagine the lights and darks of your fate against
the world?
The lights were clean, curated
Allowing for love and beauty and the innocence
of 20
While your darks…were they true? Did you ever
imagine such a day when your brush stokes
would match the strokes of the fire that blazed in
your eyes before you left this world?
Did you know? Is that why you spread the love
so deeply, the poetry so profoundly, because you
were grateful for the time?
(the wisdom so concentrated…)
I miss you every day. You managed to travel to
the depths of Truth ages before any of us, with a
love that outshined us all.

# The Exception

My words sit beneath Lao Tzu and all I can
think about is how much war has inspired the
love within me
Like a true anarchist, I rise only when provoked
with the threat of a good time
When "actualization" means fighting off the
stupidity of anything other than harmony
When peace is made a mockery of
When the currency of hatred postures itself next
to love like the pebble against the mountain who
demands a podium
No one truly believes that the two are equal,
right?
I watch as the bucks fight outside my window
and the neighbors argue for their placement of
the trash cans on the street and think,
"this must be the exception, yes?"

# Authenticity

The bulbs I tend to pale in comparison to the
bulbs that fell from the delivery truck and into
the ditch
Manicured vs natural
Which pay-per-view battle would we choose to
view?
The tended one has the structure of the centuries
of science, thoughts and methodologies and
recipients and donors,
A constant watchful eye of support and guidance
And the ditch-bulb, the mere fate of its
environment; its only hope is in its wisdom.
No one cheers for the ditch, because it doesn't
have cameras or rallies of people meddling with
their greedy hands to prune its leaves and give it
the compost of thought
And yet somehow at the conclusion if its life
when the omniscient power makes its
judgement,
and both plants approach the bench with their
respective accomplishments,
Tended-to has the grace and poise and pedigree
to present itself in every vase in America with
pride.

But only Ditch-bulb will bolt and dare to be ugly
so that it may pass on its seed for infinite
centuries, growing in all the other inevitable
ditches and cracks and abandoned homes and
whispering to the children their secrets for
immortality; daring to be authentic.

# Ice Ages

You've taken one for the team
But I've taken three
When your earthquake hits my volcano screams
How many more ice ages can we bear
Until you travel up through my spine and take
the lungs right out of my air?

# Man-Made

You lay on the floor near the fireplace seeking
warmth
As if the warmth of my heart wouldn't ignite
your dreams and desires right away
Sometimes the grey skies and the cold rain
remind me of the blazes of August nights
And your smile is the gasoline to my flame
But what is gasoline but a man-cultivated
resource that robs of the earth its millions of
years of death-in-celebration
And is that something that one could be proud to
start a fire with?
What I'd love instead is the flame that ignites
from the angered sunbeam into the sequoia
forest,
The only way that the seeds can germinate is
through the chaos and immediacy, the oldest
natural order of things.
What are we, dear love, but the culmination of
harvested-death and man made sticks created for
the sole purpose of instigating a manufactured
fire?

# Swollen Eyes

In a moment of softness does the rain ever say
"I'm sorry" as it floods through the homes made
of dust
Washing away all the old photographs and
children's toys and the journals filled with page
upon page of desire and dreams
The heavens sighing and weeping at the state of
the union of man and land
And man screams back to the sky "But I built
this pathway just for you with my sweat and
bones"
And nature replies with swollen eyes, "I didn't
need you to provide pathways for me. You see
These sunbeams always point down onto your
skin, igniting the peace and solace within
And the wind is a map that shows the trees
where their next season of kin will begin.
And the rising tides are mere love notes to the
moon who gives us our cycles and flows,
And the buds and blooms that pop up between
the mushrooms give space to hide where the
predators loom.
Dear sweet man I never asked for all of this."

And as the sun looked down she found that the
man had already turned away to discuss politics
with his neighbor.

# Faithfully as the Leaves

The wisdom to know the difference
Between a man's love and the love of nature
Is not that hard to spot.
After all, the canyons between the unruly bark of
the oak trees match the canyons between the
cells in your cheeks when you smile
And the wind whistles through the forest the
way your words whistle through my ears in the
evening,
When the bird's call dwindles and the echoes of
bats chime betwixt the hills and the sun
submerges itself along the horizon, playfully
mimicking the dolphins as they come up for air
I see the way the moon rises in your irises, full
and bright with possibilities
And I see the way your freckles match the
speckled mossy ground in the spring.
Your love comes to me as sure as the crocuses
push onward through the icy ground
Out of sight through the darknesses of winters,
but faithfully as the leaves regrow.

# Middle Way

There's a place on my street called "Alex's
Discount Store"
The lights mock me sometimes as I come home,
soft and sore
Between the aisles of tissue and beer lay my last
hopes and dreams that disappear
The fluorescent light illuminates the prices of all
my fears and vices
And all the shopkeepers and their devices
keeping their attention from nations in crisis
I envy those who can afford the treats and go
above and beyond to make sure they can eat
"Girl dinner is for the lovesick, sad and bruised"
but these days it's all for my main muse
The middle way is all I have, I whisper to myself
As one of my hands reaches for yours and one
grabs the wine off the shelf

# Nothing is as it Seems

Because my Jupiter is in alignment with the mint
leaves today as they decided to spread through
the trellis and out into the tomatoes
Nothing is as it appears to be
The bricks I laid to mark the walking path is
linear and true,
Though all of life's anecdotes say they are
supposed to be spirals or shapeless
And anyway the irrigation systems seem to be
rotting and unruly
And the timing of the sun and moon are
incorrect for the English garden plot
And the skunks and squirrels love to have lunch
at 2am when the chickens are sleeping and the
door is ajar to their feed trough
What I mean to say is, nothing is as it seems to
the human eye,
And timing is about formulating sentences in a
world of hundred-page-novels.
We see the landscape, we see the hillside and
think 'man a garden would do quite nicely here'
to feed the family and give me a hobby to allow
my own mind to collect the garbage in scented
little bags for trash day on Monday (even though

the moon doesn't care about Mondays or even
Saturdays)
But we never asked the hillside how it likes to
breathe

# My Muse

The slow emergence of warmth tickles the youth
of my cheeks
While the kin gaze at me from afar,
Upholding traditions as they listen to their little
star spout unrealized languages into the
flowerbeds,
Ethereal delights drown out the adult fights that
take place around such rites of passage
I chanted to my muse, beloved sun, gazing at the
power source through blue-green eyes
Reaching for something grander beyond the
skin's capabilities

# Calibri

I watch as the Calibri flits about and makes its
nest outside my windowsill,
Her beak holding scraps from the mattress we
threw away last year
Our infidelities and our greatest passions
powering the shelter of another
As we exchange new power dynamics the eggs
are laid and the nectar drawn
A timeless constant, cycles are. The only true
compass I've come to know is the one of the
uncertainty of the seasons
Will it be warm? Will my potatoes grow?
Will the squirrels and chipmunks allow the
berries to ripen on the vine so I can make juice
for my beloved?
Or will the rain come and wash away the seeds
and force me to wait in the grass for months as I
stare in silence and wait for the blooms that will
never come?

# Whisk me Away

Whisk me away to that grey pebble cabin
The one with the old creaky windows and
rotting doors
So I can see your beautiful eyes the way that the
rolling evergreen hills do
The rain is so quiet here and the birds sing
louder than my god forsaken inner being
And for a moment I understand.
The blades of grass whisper to the dandelions
their secrets
As the young girls braid them into crowns and
adorn each other,
And the cobblestone path draws a replica of
your smiling face asking me to come home,
The cloud-pillows agreeing and the waves
crashing into the shore exactly the same way
your bedsheets wrap around us, powerfully and
hastily with the certainty of the moon rising
once more

# Roses or Poppies

The mockingbird asked me the other day
If I use my soil to grow poppy seeds or roses
And I sighed, gazing onto the blank canvas of
my newly shined raised beds and replied:
I use my soil to grow brassicas in the cool Los
Angeles nights and cabbage in the spring,
But sometimes I use it to grow cucumbers in
July,
And its those times that the squirrels laugh and
the skunks come out to view the ridiculous
spectacle
of seeds that refuse to bend to the will of
well-balanced nitrogen and dead things even
though that could be their way of things if I had
enough straw and water and shade
A tragic affair it is, learning the language of the
seeds as they want to be translated
So I've decided to grow both poppies and roses,
To see which one can stand me

# Numbers

Sometimes I like numbers, they give me the
sanctuary of mind-knowing,
And I was told nature exists within numbers as
well,
The way the seashells spiral out of the deep
ocean sand and the way the seagulls float on the
wind waves of true north to find their way.
Sometimes even the bears sleep for seasons on
end, month after month of exact caloric usage
calculated through the ease of true rest
The numbers also help with the exact amount of
food I'll have for my family in the winter.
50 apples, 4 cows, 6 gallons of tomatoes off the
vine
But isn't it lovely to watch the squirrels eat the
avocados off the trees when they please?
To see the bees frequenting the berry blossoms
as they find them?
Is it that a line is drawn with 5, 10 or fifteen,
Or is it all the lovely experiences of life
in-between?

# Moo

I hold your fur-cheeks one last time as the salt
rivers flow from my desert-like irises onto the
harsh metal ground
Oh how I wish you would promenade with me in
the grass instead
Telling me the secrets of the pill-bugs and the
flight patterns of the butterflies,
Or how to use my chest to speak as well as
breathe,
To see through the simplest eyes and the most
neutral soul
 as you vibrate tiny worlds open with your
larynx alone
I suppose I'll just watch the sun set from my
window 8 pounds lighter
And walk in the Godless streets with cleaner
clothes
And perhaps the red-seared constellations of
conflict on my hands will disappear without a
trace
But what I do know now is my heart can
actually bleed
And unsupervised it will empty itself and turn
blue and coagulate into the memory-foam
crescent-roll shape you left behind on the couch
we bought together

# Oh Sol

I had my symposium with the sun last week
On the final day of the earthly season
When Darkness enters in its favorite
white-velvet cloak and is celebrated by the moon
and the cosmos
When the holly trees extend their welcome to
give hope and solace to the sleeping humans
underneath
'What is it that you've learned from my stay?'
He said, voice bellowing over the wolves howls
'Dear Sun, everything intends itself towards
you. You are the only one to coax the seeds out
of their slumber,
Adding color to the apple trees and golden-ray
pathways that have led me to all the homes I've
made. But tell me something oh sol, does it get
lonely shedding your power onto our days
without learning anything in return?' I say, the
same decibel as the crickets
He disappears with a glimmering sigh behind the
mountain face and in his absence I prepare a fire
with his remains

# Checkmarks and Sunbeams

My friend the coyote lurks through the high
grass and the crows hum their deep resonant
calls toward my bedroom window
An undocumented and unsolidified union of
diplomatic proportions,
The beaks tell me of danger and in return I leave
them the leftover lamb bones, olives and bread
I may have four walls but the truth is I'm just a
stranger here,
Even the ants with their anthills and the gophers
with their miles of unseen earthly tunnels know
the days of the week better than my boss does
As I add little checkmarks to my to-do list and
pickup toothpaste and soap from the fluorescent
foyers the cats clean their claws and still have
time to meet the sunbeams
Everything I know is made up,
Everything except the cherry blossoms and the
rain in June

www.ingramcontent.com/pod-product-compliance
Lightning Source LLC
Chambersburg PA
CBHW071242140726
47996CB00007B/2721